D0503672

Signs on the Way

Marvin Buckley

Dad and I are going to the hospital.

We see this sign on the way.

This sign tells us how fast
we can drive.

We see this sign on the way.

This sign tells us to stop
for other cars.

We see this sign on the way.

This sign tells us to slow down for roadwork.

We see this sign on the way.

This sign tells us what street
we are on.

We see this sign on the way.

This sign tells us we are
near the hospital.

We see this sign on the way.

This sign tells us where
to find my new baby brother.